Stress Therapy

Stress Therapy

written by
Tom McGrath

illustrated by
R.W. Alley

ONE CARING PLACE

Abbey Press

Text © 1997 by Tom McGrath
Illustrations © 1997 by St. Meinrad Archabbey
Published by One Caring Place
Abbey Press
St. Meinrad, Indiana 47577

Library of Congress Catalog Number
96-79961

ISBN 978-0-87029-301-6

Printed in the United States of America

Foreword

Stress is a natural part of everyone's life. It's the physical and emotional agitation you feel when faced with threats and opportunities. Life is filled with events—big and small, happy and sad—that bring about stress.

Since prehistoric times, the body's automatic response to stressful situations has prepared humans for fight or flight. When you encounter a stressful situation, your body produces adrenaline for enhanced energy and strength. Depending on the perceived threat, your reaction to stress can be mild (a shaky voice, sweaty palms) or severe (muscle tightness, shortness of breath, panic).

Stress serves you well when it heightens your creativity, your courage, and your sense of being alive. Stress can alert you that you're acting against your values. When you need an impetus to right a wrong, change a bad habit, or defend an important value in your life, stress can be your call to action.

But your body isn't meant to be in a constant crisis mode. While the physical changes that accompany stress are beneficial in the short run, over a long period of time unrelieved stress will lead to such problems as chronic anger, frustration, headaches, muscle strain, even heart problems.

Unrelieved stress also impairs your spiritual well-being. If you're worried and anxious, on edge and wary, you can't be open to the gentle goodness of life. It's hard to open up to love when you feel caught in a state of siege.

With its lighthearted illustrations, *Stress Therapy* helps you to recognize the stress in your life and your ways of coping with it. The book's wise and sound "rules" offer you easy-to-use strategies for stress management, so that your response to stress will be realistic, healthy, and effective.

1.

The best resource for managing stress is a fundamental faith that, beneath the apparent chaos, all is right with the world. Nurture such belief; it's a foundation on which you can build a stress-management strategy that will improve your life.

2.

The impact of stress on your life is determined not so much by what happens to you as by how you respond to it. Observe your response to situations, and you'll learn how your reactions increase or reduce the stress in your life.

3.

Some people rush from one thing to the next, so driven by ambition and the need to succeed that they've forgotten why they've filled their life with stress. Slow down. And pay attention. You may be missing the best part of living.

4.

Some people catastrophize every bump along life's highway and anticipate the worst. Don't paralyze yourself by magnifying your fears of the unknown and the uncontrollable.

5.

Some people believe life should be perfect and stress-free. This expectation only sets them up for more stress when life isn't. Take life on life's terms. Accept its ups and downs with grace and humor.

6.

Stress is in the eye (and heart) of the beholder. By changing your attitude, you can relieve your stress even when outer circumstances don't change.

7.

Some people think they should handle difficulties on their own. But if you have the wisdom to know what you need from others and the courage to ask for it, you'll ease your stress.

8.

Giving yourself compassion
and understanding lowers your
stress level. No matter who else
is on your side, you can be.

9.

When you're feeling stress, you're more vulnerable to negative self-talk, that chronic criticism echoing in your head and heart. Counter the negative voice with affirmations about your ability and self-worth. Say, "I'm talented, worthy, and loved," and believe it.

10.

Constantly trying to please
others guarantees stress. You
can respect and love others
without living your life for
them.

11.

When you start to feel anxious, ask, "How can I relax—now?" Know what stress-relieving techniques work for you, like deep breathing, putting your feet up, listening to music; then do them.

12.

"Take a deep breath" is wise advice. Become mindful of your breathing. Draw your breath slowly from deep within your abdomen. Then slowly exhale, releasing your tension and worry.

13.

Doing something for someone else is a great stress-reliever. Write a letter to a shut-in, make a phone call to a lonely neighbor, bake cookies for the new family down the block.

14.

The world looks bleak to those who are overtired. Give yourself enough sleep. Your soul will gently work to relieve your anxieties and restore your strength. Your subconscious will creatively devise solutions to your problems.

15.

Forgive others as well as yourself. Resentment and remorse waste energy on yesterday. Forgive and live today.

16.

Be in touch with your deepest beliefs and act on them. Living according to your values gives you a serenity that will serve you well through the most stressful times.

17.

Develop an attitude of gratitude. Making a list of blessings will put your worries in perspective. It's hard to be stressful when your heart is brimming with thanks.

18.

Practice the art of savoring life: the taste of a peach, the smell of morning, the sound of a lark, the sight of a sunrise, the soft feel of a puppy. Stop, look, listen.

19.

Watch what you eat, when you eat, and how. Gulping down junk food on the run is a recipe for stress and discomfort. Eating healthy food with loved ones strengthens the body and restores the soul.

20.

Laugh. A lot. Humor is a potent stress reducer. Foster a humorous view of life; be with people who bring laughter to your day.

21.

Sound health requires human touch. Get your minimum daily requirement of hugs, handshakes, and pats on the back. Sports, games, and dancing can help bring the human contact you need.

22.

Time is a precious gift you can use to reduce stress. Carve out an interruption-free, TV-free, phone-free time in your day. Allow your soul to catch up.

23.

Walking on a regular basis is a wonderful stress-buster. Long, leisurely strolls are good for your health, your heart, your mind, and your soul. Walking alone offers solitude; walking with others deepens relationships.

24.

Stress can arise when conflicting demands pull at you, such as work and family obligations. Reduce stress by planning ahead when you can, explaining the situation to those involved, asking for help to develop alternative approaches. And accept the fact that conflicts will arise.

25.

Free yourself to do what matters most in your life. You can let go of responsibilities that no longer serve their original purpose and say no to new tasks that fail to further your core goals.

26.

If work is a high-stress experience in your life, identify precisely what's causing your stress. Such circumstances as overwork, impossible deadlines, job insecurity, new technology, difficult co-workers can all increase your stress level.

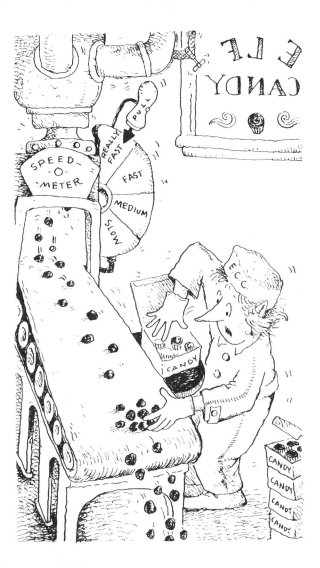

27.

Once you determine the root of your discomfort, decide if you can confront the problem head-on. If you can't change the situation, explore changing your attitude.

28.

As a preventive measure, incorporate stress-relieving techniques in your workday. Take sanity breaks. Look out the window. Walk around the block. Really taste that cup of coffee or tea.

29.

If your life and work have meaning, you'll more easily cope with stress. Two workers were asked, "What are you doing?" One answered, "I'm dragging stones from here to there." The other responded, "I'm building a cathedral!" What's your life's mission?

ELF CANDY CO.

ELF HOLLOW
HOSPITAL
VISITING HO.

30.

Do something creative every day. Stress can make you feel as if your life is shrinking. Creative activities like painting, baking, cross-stitching, or playing music expand your sense of life and send your spirit soaring.

31.

During long periods of stress, parts of your life may get neglected. Strive for balance. Take time to pray, exercise, think, read, do physical work, be alone, be with others.

32.

Some responses to stress not only make the situation worse, they can indicate deeper problems you need to address. If you react with drug or alcohol abuse, overeating, anger tantrums, self-pity, isolation, or feeling powerless and victimized, you're seriously harming your life. Seek help.

33.

If the stress you feel is too severe or lasts too long, you may not be able to fix it alone. There's nothing wrong and everything right with getting physical, spiritual, and emotional help through a difficult time.

34.

Don't underestimate how long it takes to recuperate from a crisis, loss, or other stressful event. Give yourself the time you need to grieve, rest, and restore your strength.

35.

Nature heals. The sound of birds, sparkling sunlight on a serene lake, the night sky aglow with stars all offer a balm to weary hearts and souls. When you can't go to nature, bring nature to you with an aquarium, plants, a flower box, or an indoor rock garden.

36.

Nature offers lessons about change, permanence, cycles, and harmony to illuminate your own life. Let the changing seasons teach you that hard times pass. Let the earth's strength and adaptability show you how fundamentals endure. Witness the reality of death and rebirth.

37.

Develop the trust that life will provide you with what you need. Serenity comes not in having what you want but in wanting what you have.

38.

The ultimate stress therapy is to remember the deeper truth of your life—that you are loved. When stress and its effects begin to overwhelm you, listen for the voice of God, who beckons, "Come to me when you are weary and I will give you rest."

Tom McGrath is Editorial Director for Claretian Publications, publishers of *U.S. Catholic*, *Salt of the Earth*, and *Bringing Religion Home*. He lives in Chicago with his wife, Kathleen, and his two daughters, Judy and Patti.

Illustrator for the Abbey Press Elf-help Books, **R.W. Alley** also illustrates and writes children's books. He lives in Barrington, Rhode Island, with his wife, daughter, and son. See a wide variety of his works at: www.rwalley.com.

The Story of the Abbey Press Elves

The engaging figures that populate the Abbey Press "elf-help" line of publications and products first appeared in 1987 on the pages of a small self-help book called *Be-good-to-yourself Therapy*. Shaped by the publishing staff's vision and defined in R.W. Alley's inventive illustrations, they lived out author Cherry Hartman's gentle, self-nurturing advice with charm, poignancy, and humor.

Reader response was so enthusiastic that more Elf-help Books were soon under way, a still-growing series that has inspired a line of related gift products.

The especially endearing character featured in the early books—sporting a cap with a mood-changing candle in its peak—has since been joined by a spirited female elf with flowers in her hair.

These two exuberant, sensitive, resourceful, kindhearted, lovable sprites, along with their lively elfin community, reveal what's truly important as they offer messages of joy and wonder, playfulness and co-creation, wholeness and serenity, the miracle of life and the mystery of God's love.

With wisdom and whimsy, these little creatures with long noses demonstrate the elf-help way to a rich and fulfilling life.

Elf-help Books

...adding "a little character" and a lot
of help to self-help reading!

Healing Touch Therapy	#20430
Conflict Resolution Therapy	#20391
When Your Parent Dies	#20369
Thirty Days of Grief Prayers	#20367
On the Anniversary of Your Loss	#20363
When You're Feeling Spiritually Empty	#20360
Elf-help for Coping with Cancer	#20359
Elf-help for Healing from Abuse	#20356
Elf-help for the Mother-to-Be	#20354
Believe-in-yourself Therapy	#20351
Grieving at Christmastime	#20052
Elf-help for Giving the Gift of You!	#20054
Grief Therapy	#20178
Healing Thoughts for Troubled Hearts	#20058
Take Charge of Your Eating	#20064

Peace Therapy	#20176
Friendship Therapy	#20174
Christmas Therapy (color edition) $5.95	#20175
Happy Birthday Therapy	#20181
Forgiveness Therapy	#20184
Keep-life-simple Therapy	#20185
Acceptance Therapy	#20190
Keeping-up-your-spirits Therapy	#20195
Slow-down Therapy	#20203
One-day-at-a-time Therapy	#20204
Prayer Therapy	#20206
Be-good-to-your-marriage Therapy	#20205
Be-good-to-yourself Therapy	#20255

Book price is $4.95 unless otherwise noted.
Available at your favorite gift shop or bookstore—
or directly from One Caring Place, Abbey Press
Publications, St. Meinrad, IN 47577.
Or call 1-800-325-2511.
www.carenotes.com

Notes

Notes

Notes